HYMNS OF THE FAITHFUL SERIES

LENT
EASTER

LEADERS GUIDE

WRITTEN BY

Richard Resch

CPH.
Concordia Publishing House

Contents

Series editor: Thomas J. Doyle

This publication is available in braille and in large print for the visually impaired. Write to the Library for the Blind, 1333 S. Kirkwood Rd., St. Louis, MO 63122-7295; or call 1-800-433-3954.

Introduction

The Hymns of the Faithful Bible study series provides participants the opportunity to study in-depth favorite hymns and Christian songs. This CD pack contains two of a series of six studies.

The leaders guide includes background information concerning the text and tune for some of Christendom's most beloved hymns. Each session in the leaders guide includes the following sections:

- **Textual Source(s)**–provides the scriptural sources the author used in writing the hymn.
- **The Hymn's Text**–provides information concerning the author of the hymn and the context in which the hymn was written.
- **The Hymn's Tune**–provides information concerning the tune associated with the hymn, including who wrote the tune and alernate uses of the tune.
- **Tradition about the Hymn**–describes the way in which the hymn has been used by the church.
- **The Confession of Faith Sung in This Hymn**–describes the theological truth(s) that the hymn confesses.

The study sheets are designed for use in a class or small-group setting, but may also be used by individuals for their personal devotions. Every session has a separate study sheet. Each of the reproducible study sheets includes activities and questions to guide the participant into an understanding of the basic theological truths confessed in the hymn and to assist the participant in applying these truths to life. Each study sheet includes the following sections:

- **Focus**–introduces the participant to the concepts that will be explored during the session.
- **Inform**–provides questions to guide the participant into a deeper understanding of the scriptural truths confessed in the words of the hymn. This section may be supplemented by the leader with information found in the leaders guide.
- **Connect**–provides activities and questions to help the participant apply the truth found in the words of the hymn to life.
- **Vision**–suggests activities for further devotional use of the hymn during the week to come.

In addition to the leaders guide and the study sheets, an audio CD includes a musical, sing-along version of the hymn. Use the audio CD to accompany your class or small group in singing the hymn at the beginning of each session. You may also want to play the hymn as participants arrive and/or depart from class.

May God bless the study of His Word proclaimed in the words of some of the church's favorite hymns.

Session 1

All Glory, Laud, and Honor

Textual Sources:
Matthew 21:1–11; Mark 11:1–10; Luke 19:29–38; and John 12:12–15

The Hymn's Text

This is one of the few medieval hymns whose authorship is certain. The text is ascribed to Theodulf (750–821), Bishop of Orleans, by his contemporary Lupus of Ferrieres in a letter written in 837.

"All Glory, Laud, and Honor" has a lovely story connected to it; however, the story is not true. But since the story is so attractive, it tends to live on. We do know for fact that Theodulf was imprisoned around 818 for taking part in a plot to overthrow King Louis I, a charge that Theodulf vigorously denied. John Julian writes the following account in his *Dictionary of Hymnology.*

> On Palm Sunday, 821, Louis the Pious, King of France, was at Angers and took part in the usual procession of the clergy and laity. As the procession passed the place where St. Theodulf was incarcerated he stood at the open window of his cell, and amid the silence of the people, sang this hymn which he had newly composed. The king was so much delighted with the hymn that he at once ordered St. Theodulf to be set at liberty and restored to his see; and ordained that henceforth the hymn should always be used in processions on Palm Sunday.

This story is not, however, a contemporary account; and moreover it seems clear that Louis the Pious was never in Angers after 818. It is almost certain that St. Theodulf was never really restored to his see, but that he died at Angers in 821.

Translation

The English version by the famous Greek and Latin hymn translator, John Mason Neale, appeared for the first time in 1851 in London. An additional stanza was usually a part of this text until about the 17th century when it was dropped (for obvious reasons).

> Be Thou, O Lord, the Rider,
> And we the little ass;
> That to God's Holy City
> Together we may pass.

The Hymn's Tune

The tune connected with this text has a variety of names: THEODULF, ST. THEODULF, KRONSTADT, and VALET WILL ICH DIR GEBEN. It was written by a Lutheran pastor, Melchior Teschner (1584–1635) of Silesia, at a time of great sadness in Germany (1614). This was four years before the Thirty Years War, and the country was already suffering from terrible plagues. Teschner had just become pastor at Oberpritschen when he penned this setting to be sung with Valerius Herberger's hymn for the dying, *"Valet will ich dir geben"* (Farewell I gladly bid thee).

The music associated with hymn processions on Palm Sunday was originally set to a text that spoke of longing to be in heaven and out of this troubled sphere. Nevertheless, the strong and versatile tune is able to serve both texts. But for most, it is the "All Glory, Laud, and Honor" text that comes to mind when the Teschner tune is heard.

Tradition about the Hymn

Processions on Palm Sunday were at times outdoors, with the members of the congregation waving palm branches as they processed through the city. Variations developed in certain places, such as at the Salisbury and York cathedrals. There the first four stanzas were always sung by seven boys who went to the top of the south gatehouse to sing over the procession below.

The *Lutheran Worship Agenda* gives the following rubrics:

The congregation gathers in some convenient place, the branches or fronds of palm are distributed. ... The PROCESSION into the church begins with the congregation, branches raised, following the pastor and assisting minister(s) and singing "All Glory, Laud, and Honor."

The Confession of Faith Sung in This Hymn

All of creation (*children, angels, creation, all mortals,* and *pilgrims*) raise a mighty chorus to the Redeemer King. But how much of creation really knows what this is all about? Clearly the angels do. But do many of those for whom it is happening? We have here a King who will be killed. He is surrounded by mobs watching a procession with eyes that understand "glory" as the world defines it. But the one who rides before them will find "glory" in a different way. His greatest glory will be on a cross where He will save us and provide us an eternity of glory. The King comes to receive His kingship by means of a cross.

On Palm Sunday the church waves palm branches and lifts its voice in sweet "hosannas" (save us) to the one who goes forth to win victory for us over sin, death, and the power of the devil. A profound, solemn, and explicit understanding of where this process will lead is found in the hymn "The Royal Banners Forward Go" (*LW* 103). The waving palms and the voices of children begin this great week as our Lord enters Jerusalem to die.

Session 2
Glory Be to Jesus

Textual Sources:
1 Peter 1:18–21 and Hebrews 9:11–14

The Hymn's Text

   This simple, yet profoundly beautiful devotional text is 18th-century Italian in origin, but the author is unknown. It was published for the first time in Rome in 1837. Lutheran hymnals include only six stanzas, but the original text has nine. Therefore, the word *cento* probably appears somewhere on the hymnal page, indicating that this hymn is a portion of a larger work. The term appears usually in the author credit line. The English translation associated with this text is by Edward Caswall, and it appeared for the first time in 1857. The following stanzas completed the hymn:

6. *There the fainting spirit*
   Drinks of life her fill;
   There as in a fountain
   Laves herself at will.
   (lave means to wash; to bathe)

7. *Oh, the Blood of Christ!*
   Soothes the Father's ire;
   Opens the gate of Heaven;
   Quells eternal fire.

8. *Abel's blood for vengeance*
   Pleaded to the skies;
   But the blood of Jesus
   For our pardon cries.

9. *Oft as it is sprinkled*
   On our guilty hearts,
   Satan in confusion
   Terror-struck departs.

The Hymn's Tune

   The tune is most often called WEM IN LEIDENSTAGEN. Occasionally it is called FILITZ (for the composer) or CASWALL (for the translator). Friedrich Filitz wrote this tune to be sung with a funeral text called *"Wem in Leidenstagen."* The tune appears for the first time in print in 1846. The text and tune, while not written for each other, were written at about the same time in history. How they came to be wed together we do not know, yet it is a perfect match. Text and tune serve each other well. One does not dominate the other, but they carry each other. This is one of the reasons why some hymns are loved and continue to live on in history.

Tradition about the Hymn

Unlike "All Glory, Laud, and Honor," this hymn does not automatically appear in all of the present hymnals of Christendom. Much of Christendom is uncomfortable talking, let alone singing, about sin and its consequences. We understand, though, that in order to appreciate fully the magnitude of God's love revealed in the person and work of Jesus, we must first confess the rancor of our sin.

Because of the simplicity of melody, harmony, and the text, this may be one of the most taught hymns in Christian schools and Sunday schools.

The Confession of Faith Sung in This Hymn

There is confusion in the church and in the world concerning "glory." This hymn has the word in its first line. People rarely understand "glory" as our Lord would have them understand it.

One of the strongest features of hymns is that they teach us doctrine. And this hymn teaches how our Lord would have us understand His glory. It is not a mountaintop picture of triumphant glory that is easy to view. No, this hymn speaks pointedly about the bitter pains and the spilled blood of Jesus. The end of the hymn describes heaven exalting Jesus' death and a joyous, loud swell of voices responding. The voices respond to the most important act in all history. God's people lift their voices in praise even as they speak of the suffering, torment, and dying of Jesus and proclaim the cross as the highest glory.

O Sacred Head, Now Wounded

Textual Sources:
Psalm 22:6–8; Isaiah 50:6; Matthew 27:28–31; and John 19:1–6

The Hymn's Text

"O Sacred Head, Now Wounded" is one of the most famous and beloved hymns. It therefore appears in virtually every Christian hymnal. In fact, most Christians would have a difficult time imagining Holy Week without singing this hymn. Four very big names are usually associated with the hymn: Bernard of Clairvaux, Paul Gerhardt, Hans Leo Hassler, and Johann Sebastian Bach.

Until quite recently, it was believed that Bernard of Clairvaux (1091–1153) authored this sublime text, which is part of a much larger work. Unfortunately, the author is not known, even though most hymnals credit Clairvaux. Nevertheless, in the magnificent larger work there are seven sections, and each addresses a different member of Christ's body languishing on the cross, one at a time: the feet, the knees, the hands, the side, the breast, the heart, and the head.

Translation

Paul Gerhardt (1607–76) is best known as the hymn writer who taught the church how to sing the theology of the cross. But in "O Sacred Head, Now Wounded," his role was translator of an existing text. Pastor Gerhardt took the last part of the Latin poem, the part that addresses the head, and wrote a 10-stanza hymn in German. This was first published in 1656. The enormous popularity of Gerhardt's German version was carried into numerous English versions. Philip Schaff writes:

> *This classical hymn has shown an imperishable vitality in passing from the Latin into the German, and from the German into the English, and proclaiming in three tongues, and in the name of three confessions—the Catholic, Lutheran, and Reformed—with equal effect, the dying love of our Savior and our bound-less indebtedness to him. (Christ in Song, 1869)*

The Hymn's Tune

The tune, HERZLICH TUT MICH VERLANGEN (also PASSION CHORALE), is by Hans Leo Hassler and was first set to a funeral hymn called *"Herzlich tut mich verlangen."* The tune name comes from this funeral hymn, not from

Gerhardt's text. The tune appears for the first time coupled with Gerhardt's 10-stanza hymn in Johann Cruger's *Praxis pietatis melica* (1656). The Hassler version is highly rhythmic.

Johann Sebastian Bach (1685–1750) used this melody often in his works, including it five times in the *St. Matthew Passion* and twice in the *Christmas Oratorio*, and it is found in five of his cantatas. The Bach version is very simple rhythmically and is the version that appears most frequently in the hymnals.

The Confession of Faith Sung in This Hymn

"What language can I borrow to thank You, dearest friend?" With these words, we make use of some of the most eloquent language to thank our dearest Friend, Jesus, for what He has accomplished for us through His death.

As we view and behold the extreme suffering of our Lord, we are left speechless. And yet we are not speechless, for we sing in a profound way exactly the truth of His passion. We may be overcome emotionally by the truth, the reality of what we sing in these words.

In a time when people are so reluctant to look at sin and its consequences, this text may come as a shock. There is no smoothing-over here. It would be easier for us to look the other way. The desire to take the easy route and look away explains why this hymn has lost some of its popularity in recent days.

Christ's torment is real. The reason for His torment is disclosed: "all this for **my** transgression" (emphasis added). We sing this hymn with repentant and grateful hearts, rejoicing in the eternal life His torment won for us.

Session 4

Go to Dark Gethsemane

Textual Sources:
Lamentations 3:19; Matthew 26:36–39; and Luke 24:18

The Hymn's Text

Many believe that the author of this text, James Montgomery (1771–1854), ranks with Charles Wesley and Isaac Watts in his contribution to English hymnody. He started writing poetry at the age of 10 and as an adult was a journalist by profession. He authored about 300 hymns, including the following: "Angels from the Realms of Glory," "Hail to the Lord's Anointed," "In the Hour of Trial," "Come to Calvary's Holy Mountain," "To Your Temple, Lord, I Come," "Songs of Praise the Angels Sang." In addition to his hymns, he wrote poetry that voiced a strong stand against slavery.

Montgomery's original version of "Go to Dark Gethsemane" was written and published in 1820 in *A Selection of Psalms and Hymns for Public and Private Use*. Two years later he published the version found in most hymnals. The following is an example of the type of changes he made.

Original Stanza 2	Final Stanza 2
See Him at the judgment hall,	*Follow to the judgment hall,*
Beaten, bound, reviled, arraign'd:	*View the Lord of life arraigned;*
See Him meekly bearing all!	*Oh, the wormwood and the gall!*
Love to man His soul sustain'd!	*Oh, the pangs His soul sustained!*
Shun not suffering, shame or loss;	*Shun not suff'ring, shame, or loss;*
Learn of Christ to bear the cross.	*Learn from Him to bear the cross.*

Many hymnals omit stanza 4. Why might this be? Perhaps because stanza 4 clearly sings of Easter. This is unique for a passion hymn. While many Lenten hymns end with death, it is rare for a Lenten hymn to take the solemn passion worshiper to the empty tomb. Referring to the shortened versions, Bailey lists "the lessons one may learn from the three final incidents in Jesus' life: Gethsemane—learn the spirit of prayer; the Praetorium—learn how to bear the cross; Calvary—learn how to die" (*The Gospel in Hymns*). Fred Precht rightly adds, "One wonders at the omission of the greatest and final lesson: the Resurrection—learn how to live anew!"

The Hymn's Tune

The name for the tune most commonly associated with· Montgomery's text is GETHSEMANE. Other possible names for the same tune include PETRA, AHALON, or REDHEAD NO. 76. It seems that the composer, Richard Redhead (1820–1901), did not name his tunes. Tunes were therefore assigned a number. The tune GETHSEMANE first appeared as NO. 76 in Redhead's *Church Hymn Tunes, Ancient and Modern* (1853) with the text for "Rock of Ages, Cleft for Me."

The Hymn's Tradition

Without a doubt, this is a beloved hymn. "Go to Dark Gethsemane" is unique, not just because it takes the singer to Easter, but because it provides a sense of movement. You go, you watch, you follow, you view, you learn, and you climb. You are involved as this text places you there to behold what happened for you on the cross. The appropriately mournful and simple tune helps give the sense of a solemn procession.

The Confession of Faith Sung in This Hymn

In four brief stanzas, we are able to sing of the complete passion account of Jesus. And as we sing, we rehearse again what "It is finished!" means for us. Yet in Montgomery's text we do more than simply rehearse facts, for the words apply the passion to our lives.

Session 5

I Know That My Redeemer Lives

Textual Sources:
Job 19:25–27; John 14:2–4; and Hebrews 7:23–25

The Hymn's Text

There is little written about the background and traditions that have developed surrounding "I Know That My Redeemer Lives." The text by Samuel Medley (1738–99) first appeared in George Whitefield's *Psalms and Hymns* in 1775. Medley was a Baptist minister, first in Hertfordshire, and later in Liverpool, England. It was originally a nine-stanza hymn.

The Hymn's Tune

The well-known tune is called DUKE STREET. It was written by John Hatton. The somewhat strange tune name, "DUKE STREET," has its source in the fact that for a time Hatton lived on Duke Street in Windle Township in Lancaster, England. (An aside: The composer of a tune has always been free to choose a name for the tune.) The tune DUKE STREET first appeared in print in 1793, where it was wed to Joseph Addison's paraphrase of Psalm 19: "When All Your Mercies, O My God."

Tradition about the Hymn

"I Know That My Redeemer Lives" fits well under several different topical headings in a hymnal: "Christian Hope," "Death and Burial," "Easter," and "Easter/Resurrection." Including this hymn in the "Death and Burial" and "Christian Hope" sections of a hymnal enables this wonderful text to be sung at funerals and memorial services, providing an excellent witness of faith.

The Confession of Faith Sung in This Hymn

It is amazing how much we sing on Easter Sunday about our own death. A brief perusal of the Easter hymns will show that our own mortality is mentioned often. Such singing, however, does not transfer gloom and doom to a joyous festival. Rather it connects our last moments on earth with the truth and certainty of our resurrection: because He lives, I too will live.

Every word of the hymn offers comfort and assurance. The text takes what God has done in and through Christ and applies it to our lives, our fears, and even our tears. A great strength of this hymn is that it connects God's action on our behalf to our lives, our physical deaths, and our eternal lives in heaven. "I Know That My Redeemer Lives" proclaims boldly the Gospel. Every stanza clearly focuses on what God has done for us through Jesus. This is what people need to hear as they contemplate their own deaths or the death of loved ones.

The words of this hymn bring comfort to both the deathbed and the funeral service. To hear the following words as you are dying is to receive the greatest comfort:

He lives to silence all my fears;
He lives to wipe away my tears;
He lives to calm my troubled heart;
He lives all blessings to impart.

As grieving family and friends sing together these words at a memorial service, they confess emphatically where their loved one is and where they too will go:

He lives and grants me daily breath;
He lives, and I shall conquer death;
He lives my mansion to prepare;
He lives to bring me safely there.

Stanzas 1 and 2 and stanza 8 form bookends of confession that can only be sung by children of Christ. Those children sing these words often at very difficult times, with tears in their eyes, but with a total confidence that they sing truth.

Session 6

At the Lamb's High Feast We Sing

Textual Sources:
Exodus 12:21–23; 14:22; Matthew 26:26–29;
1 Corinthians 5:6–8; and Revelation 5:11–13

The Hymn's Text

This 17th-century Latin office hymn is a revision of a much older Latin text that dates between A.D. 500 and 800. The original first stanza speaks of those clothed in white robes at the high feast, a reference to those baptized at the Easter Vigil on Easter Eve.

The hymn provides a series of striking images of Christ: He is at the same time the Host of the feast (who provides the sacrifices), the Priest (who offers the sacrifice), and the Victim (the sacrifice itself). Stanza 3 refers to the Passover account in Exodus 12 and 14 and to the New Testament reference from 1 Corinthians 5:7–8.

The current translation was prepared and published in 1849 by a Scottish lawyer, Robert Campbell.

The Hymn's Tune

This glorious text has been sung to a number of different melodies. But all the present American Lutheran hymnals have wed the text with the strong and fitting tune, SONNE DER GERECHTIGKEIT.

The tune SONNE DER GERECHTIGKEIT has a musical factor that makes it a bit more complex than the typical hymn. It is a factor common in Latin hymnody called the "melisma." A melisma occurs when two or more notes are sung to the same syllable. Melismas occur in the first and second phrases of this hymn. They are indicated on the page by a slur over the notes. This was a common musical device in Gregorian chant and is presented here in its most simplified form with a four-note maxim. This factor adds to the beauty of the hymn.

Tradition about the Hymn

"At the Lamb's High Feast We Sing" is an example of an ancient text that has enjoyed great acceptance during the last 30 years.

The hymn concludes with a doxological stanza—a confession of praise to the Father, Son, and Holy Spirit. Doxological stanzas are common characteristics of Latin hymns, even those that focus on the passion.

The reason for the doxological stanza dates back to Ambrose (340–97), Bishop of Milan, who used hymns to battle, to reinforce, and to teach the doctrine of the Trinity during the Arian controversy (a heresy that denied the trinitarian nature of God).

The Confession of Faith Sung in This Hymn

In this hymn the church raises the roof in a full-throated song about the victory won for her by the Lamb. What is the "feast" referred to here? There is considerable debate over that question, and the answer is usually revealed by where this hymn is placed in a hymnal. Some have included it in the "Lord's Supper" section, some in the "Easter" section, and one has assigned it to "Maundy Thursday."

While some do not believe that it is appropriate to have such a splash of Alleluias and Easter triumph during Holy Week on Maundy Thursday, many see the "feast" presented here in the richest sense, including both the festival of the resurrection of our Lord and the feast offered again and again in His holy Supper.